MORNING
MOTIVATION
Inspirational Quotes

START YOUR DAY WITH POSITIVITY

ALLISON AND AARON TASK

**ROCKRIDGE
PRESS**

Copyright © 2021 by Rockridge Press, Emeryville, California

No part of this publication may be reproduced, stored in a retrieval system, or transmitted in any form or by any means, electronic, mechanical, photocopying, recording, scanning, or otherwise, except as permitted under Sections 107 or 108 of the 1976 United States Copyright Act, without the prior written permission of the Publisher. Requests to the Publisher for permission should be addressed to the Permissions Department, Rockridge Press, 6005 Shellmound Street, Suite 175, Emeryville, CA 94608.

Limit of Liability/Disclaimer of Warranty: The Publisher and the author make no representations or warranties with respect to the accuracy or completeness of the contents of this work and specifically disclaim all warranties, including without limitation warranties of fitness for a particular purpose. No warranty may be created or extended by sales or promotional materials. The advice and strategies contained herein may not be suitable for every situation. This work is sold with the understanding that the Publisher is not engaged in rendering medical, legal, or other professional advice or services. If professional assistance is required, the services of a competent professional person should be sought. Neither the Publisher nor the author shall be liable for damages arising herefrom. The fact that an individual, organization, or website is referred to in this work as a citation and/or potential source of further information does not mean that the author or the Publisher endorses the information the individual, organization, or website may provide or recommendations they/it may make. Further, readers should be aware that websites listed in this work may have changed or disappeared between when this work was written and when it is read.

For general information on our other products and services or to obtain technical support, please contact our Customer Care Department within the United States at (866) 744-2665, or outside the United States at (510) 253-0500.

Rockridge Press publishes its books in a variety of electronic and print formats. Some content that appears in print may not be available in electronic books, and vice versa.

TRADEMARKS: Rockridge Press and the Rockridge Press logo are trademarks or registered trademarks of Callisto Media Inc. and/or its affiliates, in the United States and other countries, and may not be used without written permission. All other trademarks are the property of their respective owners. Rockridge Press is not associated with any product or vendor mentioned in this book.

Interior and Cover Designer: Regina Stadnik
Art Producer: Janice Ackerman
Editor: Sean Newcott
Production Editor: Holland Baker
Production Manager: Martin Worthington

Illustration: Courtesy of Shutterstock

Paperback ISBN: 978-1-63807-362-8
eBook ISBN: 978-1-63878-028-1
R0

For Clementine, Zevin,

Abraham, and Davida.

May you enjoy each sunrise.

INTRODUCTION

We're so glad you are reading *Morning Motivation*. It's our privilege to write a book filled with inspiring ideas from a great variety of thinkers and doers from around the world, across time, *and* that can be used practically as part of your morning routine.

Inspiration can come from a wide assortment of sources and everyone finds it in their own way. Some people want (and need) a kick in the pants, while others prefer a more gentle nudge. This book contains quotes to stimulate you mentally. A good quote connects you to others and helps your inspiration take flight. When you read them, sit with them for a moment. Consider who said the quote, and try to put it in the context of the speaker's life—and your own. As you go through the book, you may find yourself inspired by quotes with similar themes—or people with similar styles.

In her coaching practice, Allison shares inspiring quotes with clients to shift their thinking, stimulate their creativity, or help ground an idea. As a journalist, Aaron knows a good quote from a reliable source helps move a story forward and makes the piece more relatable to the reader.

In addition to quotes from great thinkers, we also wrote research-based inspiring insights, and you can use these tools to invite more motivation and find greater satisfaction in your life.

Henry Ward Beecher called morning "the rudder of the day," and we agree, so we hope that you will use this book as part of your morning routine.

We are morning people. We're typically asleep by 10 p.m. and up before 6 a.m., but we haven't always been this way. Three years into our marriage, we found ourselves with four children, three of whom were under two years old. Without family members nearby who could help and with two careers underway, we needed to figure out how to set ourselves up to succeed as people, parents, and partners.

Today, we go to sleep when the kids do. We've traded booze and Netflix for the sunrise, and instead of waking with the alarm, we wake with the birds. Whether we're exercising, having an important conversation, or writing this book, our morning time becomes a sacred space for thinking, connecting, and being productive.

That's our story, which of course is different from yours. Whatever your situation or station in life, it can be so beneficial to create time and space for yourself in the morning. It's a perfect opportunity to contemplate the wisdom of others.

You have great things to contribute to the world. We need you up and at it, and this book will help you get there.

Carpe diem,
Allison and Aaron Task

"One key to success
is to have lunch at the
time most people have
breakfast."

—Robert Brault

"Cherish your visions and your dreams, as they are the children of your soul, the blueprints of your ultimate achievements."

—Napoleon Hill

"If you make your bed every morning, you will have accomplished the first task of the day. If you can't do the little things right, you will never be able to do the big things right."

—William H. McRaven

"There are no shortcuts to any place worth going."

—Beverly Sills

"When you come out of
the storm, you won't be the same
person who walked in.
That's what this storm's
all about."

—Haruki Murakami

"When adversity strikes, that's when you have to be the most calm. Take a step back, stay strong, stay grounded, and press on."

—LL Cool J

Write a letter today and address it to yourself 10 years from now. Let yourself know what matters to you now, and what you think will matter then. Write down your dreams, your aspirations, and your hopes for the experiences you'll have, the people you'll meet, the accomplishments you'll achieve.

You will go through significant changes over the next 10 years; some you can prepare for and some you cannot fathom. Some changes will be superficial, some profound. Speak kindly and compassionately to yourself, and in an understanding way about some of the difficulties you may experience. Imagine who will enter and who may leave your life. What do you want those changes to be? Perhaps this exercise will motivate you to remove some nonworking parts of your life that you've been tolerating.

To complete this letter, write a list of 10 experiences you'd like to have in the next 10 years. Then, seal the envelope and add the date when you can open it. Dream big.

"And what is a weed? A plant whose virtues have not yet been discovered."

—Ralph Waldo Emerson

". . . you are the sunshine to those who look up to you, and they are your sunbathers . . . so glow brightly."

—Bodhi Smith

"Positive thinking will let you do everything better than negative thinking will."

—Zig Ziglar

"I don't wait for inspiration; inspiration always waits for me."

—Akiane Kramarik

"You're all geniuses and you're all beautiful. You don't need anybody to tell you who you are or what you are."

—John Lennon

"Oh, but you know, you do not achieve anything without trouble, ever."

—Margaret Thatcher

Practice wordless connection with another person. Sit across from someone you know and trust and hold eye contact. Do this for one minute (set a timer). You may laugh, feel self-conscious, or be uncomfortable. That's fine and totally normal. It's a bit awkward, isn't it? When the minute is over, stop and share how the experience went. Then redo the exercise for two minutes. After those two minutes, take a break and discuss how it felt this time. Try it once more for three minutes and discuss how it felt after.

Observe how your ability to complete the exercise changes as you get used to it. Observe how you feel about the other person, how you are able to "see" them without exchanging words or ideas.

Keep the experience of this exercise with you as you go throughout your day and week. Practice deepening your connection without the distraction of words. Feel another person, see another person, connect with another person. Do not be distracted or motivated by sharing ideas with them, rather share and simply appreciate another person's presence.

"As the area
of our knowledge
grows, so too does
the perimeter of our
ignorance."

—Neil deGrasse Tyson

"I look back on my life like a good day's work—it was done and I feel satisfied with it . . . life is what we make it, always has been, always will be."

—Grandma Moses

"To take what there *is*, and use it, without waiting forever in vain for the preconceived— to dig deep into the actual and get something out of *that*— this doubtless is the right way to live."

—Henry James

"If they don't give you a seat at the table, bring a folding chair."

—Shirley Chisholm

"*Everything you need, you already have. You are complete right now, you are a whole, total person, not an apprentice person on the way to someplace else.*"

—Wayne Dyer

"Fight for the things that you care about, but do it in a way that will lead others to join you."

—Ruth Bader Ginsburg

You can actively cultivate feelings of love by taking care of another living being. Consider adopting a life, whether it's planting a tree in a part of the world that needs it, or in your own community. Adopt a pet or put out birdseed for birds in your neighborhood.

Consider other ways you might care for another living being. Perhaps it's visiting a nursing home and reading to residents, or bringing games to children who are hospitalized and playing with them. Think of areas in your life where you have availability to invite another person to receive your love and care. What might that look like?

We know that the gift of love pays dividends to the gift giver as well as the recipient. Reach out and find another living being to love and care for.

"To be or not
to be is not a question
of compromise. Either you
be or you don't be."

—Golda Meir

"Difficulties break some men but make others. No axe is sharp enough to cut the soul of a sinner who keeps on trying, one armed with the hope that he will rise and win in the end."

—Nelson Mandela

"Live on the east side of the
mountain. It's the sunrise side,
not the sunset side. It is the side
to see the day that is coming, not
to see the day that has gone."

—Tom Lea

"... watch your actions, they become your habits; watch your habits, they become your character ..."

—Frank Outlaw

"Those who mind don't
matter and those
who matter don't mind."

—Percy Morris

"And all I'm saying is, see, what a wonderful world it would be if only we'd give it a chance."

—Louis Armstrong

How often do you really *feel* the weather? How often do you say, *no, thank you,* to an air-conditioned space and really feel the heat? Or run out *into* the rain?

Ever wonder why all those great movie scenes happen in the rain? It's because rain is a release. We all feel the buildup of a rainstorm— especially on those hot, humid days. A good downpour can drop the temperature 10 degrees in a short period of time. If you're always running away from the heat, you can't fully enjoy the sublime refreshment of jumping into a lake on a hot summer day.

Put yourself in nature, however you can and feel comfortable, in all kinds of weather—and connect with it. It will help you feel more alive.

"Every time you choose to do the *easy* thing, instead of the *right* thing, you are shaping your identity, becoming the type of person who does what's easy, rather than what's right."

—Hal Elrod

"... no important endeavor that required innovation was done without risk ... in whatever you're doing, failure is an option, but fear is not ..."

—James Cameron

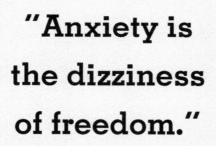

"Anxiety is
the dizziness
of freedom."

—Søren Kierkegaard

"Because it is easier to say 'I can't' than 'I can,' or at least 'I can try,' many people go through life unaware of untapped strength, even untapped ability."

—Eleanor Roosevelt

"It is, as a rule, far more important *how* [people] pursue their occupation than *what* the occupation is which they select."

—Louis Brandeis

"Success is not coming to you, you must come to it."

—Marva Collins

To paraphrase John F. Kennedy's famous quote: Ask not what your life can do for you, ask what you can do with your life.

Adopt an attitude of service each day whenever you can. Instead of looking for the job you want, or finding a city or town that you want to live in, consider seeking a life built on service.

If you want to trade the pursuit of your own desires for contributing through service, ask yourself: Is there a community that I can positively impact? How can I use my skills to help this community? If I dream big, what could the impact be when I use my skills?

The people quoted in this book worked hard at their craft. That's why we know their names. They took their natural skills and gifts to the next level, frequently in service to others.

"A life is not important except in the impact it has on other lives."

—Jackie Robinson

"I think if you do something and it turns out pretty good, then you should go do something else wonderful, not dwell on it for too long. Just figure out what's next."

—Steve Jobs

"Sometimes you have to
let go of the picture of what you
thought life would be like and
learn to find joy in the story you
are actually living."

—Rachel Marie Martin

"I can accept failure. Everyone fails at something. But I can't accept not trying."

—Michael Jordan

"Let us make our future now, and let us make our dreams tomorrow's reality."

—Malala Yousafzai

"Take every minute, one at a time. Don't be fooled by a perfect sea at any given moment. Accept and rise to whatever circumstance presents itself. Be in it full tilt, your best self. Summon your courage, your true grit."

—Diana Nyad

In addition to working hard, the most successful people also work smart. People who construct goals in concrete terms are 50 percent more likely to be confident and attain their goals and 32 percent more likely to feel in control of their lives. Many do this by using so-called SMART goals, setting objectives that are:

SPECIFIC

MEASURABLE

ATTAINABLE

RELEVANT

TIME-BOUND

SMART goals are often used to help push people to innovate at the highest level. Be they "SMART," "SMARTER," or some other name, setting goals like this will help you establish objectives that are attainable, while simultaneously pushing the limits of your potential. As a result, you'll be more likely to both hit your goals and expand the reach of how far you believe you can go.

"Decision is a sharp knife that cuts clear and straight and lays bare the fat and the lean; indecision, a dull one that hacks and tears and leaves ragged edges behind it."

—John Graham

"Just because you have a choice, it doesn't mean that any of them *has* to be right."

—Norton Juster

"*Never grow a wishbone, daughter, where your backbone ought to be.*"

—Clementine Paddleford

"Don't fear failure.
Not failure, but low aim,
is the crime. In great
attempts it is glorious
even to fail."

—Bruce Lee

"We're going to the moon because it's in the nature of the human being to face challenges . . . We're required to do these things just as salmon swim upstream."

—Neil Armstrong

"Half of the failures in life come from pulling one's horse when he is leaping."

—Julius Charles Hare & Augustus William Hare

If you're a parent, caretaker, or work with children, you may have heard that it's better to applaud a kid's effort versus telling them they're "smart" or "talented." Why is that?

Students who've been told they're "smart" often struggle with difficult problems. Because they identify as "smart" or "gifted," they become stressed and frustrated when the answers don't come easily. Conversely, students who've been praised for their hard work tend to be more persistent in trying to find the right answer, and their sense of self isn't harmed if they can't.

Ultimately, this boils down to a sense of control. Whether in school, work, or athletics, people who feel a greater sense of control tend to be more successful.

There are probably many aspects of your life you can't control, so don't waste time and energy focusing on them. Instead, find areas where you can exert control. Taking ownership of even small things, like what time you get up in the morning, will set the tone for the rest of your day and, ultimately, your life.

"Being defeated is often a temporary condition. Giving up is what makes it permanent."

—Marilyn vos Savant

"I am not
discouraged, because
every wrong attempt
discarded is another
step forward."

—Thomas Edison

"The positive thinker sees the invisible, feels the intangible, and achieves the impossible."

—Winston Churchill

"Judge each day
not by the harvest
you reap but by the
seeds you plant."

—William Arthur Ward

"The way we see the problem
is the problem."

—Stephen Covey

"In life, there is no gift as overlooked or as inevitable as failure."

—David Goggins

Jumping into frigid water is a New Year's tradition for some, and serious athletes use ice baths to recover from intense workouts. As a December 2020 meta-analysis study shows, cold-water swimming can have numerous health benefits, including:

BETTER CARDIOVASCULAR PERFORMANCE, including a "decrease in triglycerides . . . and a lower concentration of homocysteine," which can lead to heart disease.

RELEASE OF BENEFICIAL HORMONES such as catecholamines, insulin, thyroid-stimulating hormone (TSH), and adrenocorticotropic hormone (ACTH).

IMPROVED IMMUNITY, resulting in fewer infections and "an improvement in general well-being in swimmers who suffered from rheumatism, fibromyalgia, or asthma."

PSYCHOLOGICAL BENEFITS, because cold-water swimming "activates the sympathetic nervous system and increases the concentration of norepinephrine and beta-endorphin."

WARNING: There are also serious risks, especially for people with high blood pressure, so consult your doctor before taking the plunge.

"Develop enough courage so that you can stand up for yourself and then stand up for somebody else."

—Maya Angelou

"A very great vision is needed, and the [person] who has it must follow it as the eagle seeks the deepest blue of the sky."

—Crazy Horse

"It seems to me what is called for is an exquisite balance between two conflicting needs: the most skeptical scrutiny of all hypotheses that are served up to us and at the same time a great openness to new ideas."

—Carl Sagan

"This is my charge to everyone: We have to be better, we have to love more and hate less. Listen more and talk less. It is our responsibility to make this world a better place."

—Megan Rapinoe

"Things can get out of a black hole, both to the outside, and possibly to another universe. So if you feel you are in a black hole, don't give up. There's a way out."

—Stephen Hawking

"I never wanted
to lose, never thought
I would, but the thing
that matters is
how you lose."

—Muhammad Ali

Scientists have long known the benefits of playtime for children and adolescents. "Play is essential to development because it contributes to the cognitive, physical, social, and emotional well-being of children and youth," according to the *Journal of the American Academy of Pediatrics*.

But what about the rest of us? Other than clinical "play therapy" for people with mental or physical ailments, the value of play for adults is often overlooked. This is particularly unfortunate because many adults are suffering in our hard-charging culture, which tends to look down on "downtime."

As renowned pediatrician and psychoanalyst Donald Woods Winnicott wrote in the late 1960s, "it is in playing and only in playing that the individual child *or adult* is able to be creative and to use the whole personality, and it is only in being creative the individual discovers the self." (Italics added.)

So whatever "play" means to you—be it tennis, Scrabble, cards, painting, or riding a bike—go have fun! This intentional act of creativity supports your self-discovery, which in turn helps you feel inspired to create the future self you'd like to be.

"If you have an opportunity to accomplish something that will make things better for someone coming behind you, and you don't do that, you are wasting your time on this earth."

—Roberto Clemente

"Keep away from people who try to belittle your ambitions. Small people always do that, but the really great make you feel that you, too, can become great."

—Mark Twain

"The difference between a successful person and others is not a lack of strength, not a lack of knowledge, but rather a lack of will."

—Vince Lombardi

"Learn the alchemy true
human beings know:
the moment you accept
what troubles you've
been given, the door
will open."

—Rumi

"The quality of your attention determines the quality of other people's thinking."

—Nancy Kline

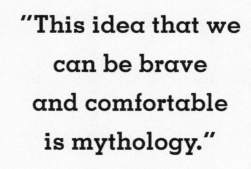

"This idea that we
can be brave
and comfortable
is mythology."

—Brené Brown

If you've ever gone on vacation, you've probably experienced the benefits of breaking routine. "Getting away from it all" can help your body, mind, and spirit.

The good news is you don't have to go to Cabo, Paris, or anywhere else to enjoy similar benefits; even better, you don't have to spend any money. Just changing how you do "routine" things can inspire new ways of thinking—all in the comfort of your home. Consider, for example, taking a different route to school or work, or using your nondominant hand to brush your teeth, or moving your computer mouse to the "other" side of the computer.

As of this writing, scientists are still trying to determine why and how this works, but "even a slight change in otherwise routine activities can make you think in a different way," according to the Alzheimer's and Dementia Resource Center (ADRC).

Start tinkering with everyday activities and stimulate inspiration.

"The best years of your life are the ones in which you decide your problems are your own. You do not blame them on your mother, the ecology, or the president. You realize that you control your own destiny."

—Albert Ellis

"... it is not yet too late to be the person you thought you could be."

—Janaya Future Khan

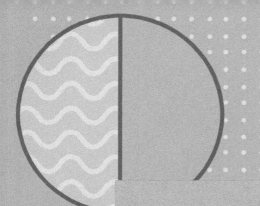

"I can always make another dollar but I can't make another day."

—Robert Kiyosaki

"Your level of success
will rarely exceed the level
of your personal development,
because success is something
you attract by the person
you become."

—Jim Rohn

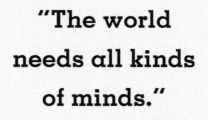

"The world
needs all kinds
of minds."

—Temple Grandin

"Imagination is more important than knowledge. For knowledge is limited, whereas imagination embraces the entire world, stimulating progress, giving birth to evolution."

—Albert Einstein

Do you use caffeine to wake up in the morning? Have you consumed alcohol or THC to help you feel more creative? Many people use drugs to feel a certain way. Drugs can be effective. And, if overused, they can lead to problems or addiction.

Hormones are natural drugs in our system. Each hormone has a different effect, providing a different "rush." Oxytocin gives you that cuddly "love" feeling (think: mommy and baby), while dopamine gives you the motivation to pursue, helping you find your courage to ask someone on a date. Serotonin lifts your mood when you achieve something difficult, like when that person says "yes" to a date.

You can cultivate your hormone response and probably already do. Have you ever watched a tearjerker because you're in the mood for a "good cry"? When watching, you put thoughts in your head that lead to physiological feelings that you tag as emotions. And who hasn't turned a garbage can into a basketball hoop when it's time to clean up? By gamifying your chores, you release dopamine, which helps you focus on a goal until it's completed.

Be aware of your hormones, and choose a desired effect, naturally.

"For there is always light, if only we're brave enough to see it."

—Amanda Gorman

"How ironic that the difficult times we fear might ruin us are the very ones that can break us open and help us blossom into who we were meant to be."

—Elizabeth Lesser

"Instead of doing the thing you *like* to do, choose to do the thing you need to work on. The thing that scares you."

—Robin Arzón

"Some people regard discipline as a chore. For me, it is a kind of order that sets me free to fly."

—Julie Andrews

"A peacock that
rests on its feathers is
just another turkey."

—Dolly Parton

"This life is mine alone. So I have stopped asking people for directions to places they've never been."

—Glennon Doyle

Can you proactively cultivate inspiration? Of course you can! Just like lightning rods can attract lightning, you can proactively encourage your creative energy to strike. Artists, for example, actively court creativity and inspiration, and often take retreats to find the mental space to create.

How (and why) do these retreats work?

COMMUNITY: By engaging with a group of like-minded people, as much or as little as you like, you feel the benefits of community.

SHIFTING LANDSCAPES, SHIFTING MINDS: Retreats remove you from routine, shifting your environment to a more relaxing, and typically natural, setting.

NO CHORES: Creative thinking flows more freely when duties or worries such as cooking, cleaning, laundry, walking the dog, etc., are removed.

By creating a situation in which you are able to harness the magic of the retreat, you will be actively courting inspiration for your own projects. And by creating a retreat environment without the retreat price tag, you'll have more money to put toward your inspired endeavors.

"Enjoy the little things in life, for one day, you may look back and realize they were the big things."

—Robert Brault

"Games make us happy
because they are hard work
that we choose for ourselves,
and it turns out that almost
nothing makes us happier
than good, hard work."

—Jane McGonigal

"People are going to give their opinions about you . . . Some people are going to make fun of you, no matter what. So you might as well do whatever you want and enjoy it."

—Austin Mahone

"Your life is not static. Every decision, setback, or triumph is an opportunity to identify the seeds of truth that make you the wondrous human being that you are."

—Oprah Winfrey

"Life is right now. It's not a morbid realization, it's exciting. I find that feeling of time constraint very liberating. Nobody has an answer. We all die in the end. So come on. Let's do something now."

—Chris Martin

"Tell me what
you value and I might
believe you, but show
me your calendar and
your bank statement, and
I'll show you what you
really value."

—Peter Drucker

Dogs do it. Cats do it. Even people who hate exercise do it. Everybody stretches, sometimes first thing in the morning just to "work out the kinks."

Many doctors recommend stretching because it "promotes flexibility and helps your joints maintain a healthy range of motion," which in turn reduces pain and the chance of injury, according to Harvard Medical School.

And stretching isn't just good for the body. It also helps your mind. Numerous academic studies have shown the mental and physical benefits of yoga, which helps oxygenate your blood and release endorphins. And there's more good news.

A Spanish study found "a short programme of stretching exercises . . . was effective for reducing levels of anxiety, bodily pain and exhaustion, and for raising levels of vitality, mental health, general health and flexibility."

In other words, you don't have to join an ashram or spend hours turning yourself into a pretzel to reap the rewards. When it comes to stretching, a little bit goes a long way!

"The thing that is really hard, and really amazing, is giving up on being perfect and beginning the work of becoming yourself."

—Anna Quindlen

"I was taught to strive not because there were any guarantees of success but because the act of striving is in itself the only way to keep faith with life."

—Madeleine Albright

"You don't get to choose how you're going to die. Or when. You can only decide how you're going to live. Now."

—Joan Baez

"Truth-tellers are not always palatable. There is a preference for candy bars."

—Gwendolyn Brooks

"All things are possible
until they are proved
impossible—and even
the impossible may only
be so, as of now."

—Pearl S. Buck

"I think we live a lot of our lives without joy. And I think loving what you're doing while you're doing it is really important."

—Veronica Chambers

Have you ever wanted to try something new but felt embarrassed or scared, or just didn't know how to get started? Whether it's going off the high dive, learning another language, or making a new recipe, it pays to listen to your inner adventurer.

Seeking new and novel experiences helps us live longer, healthier lives. Learning new skills releases dopamine and creates new neural pathways in the midbrain. The technical term for this is neophilia.

Neophilia is real . . . and it's fantastic! Just don't confuse a desire for novel experiences with impulsivity, which can lead to rash choices. Instead, be open to trying new things and look before you leap.

Over time you'll see that old dogs can not only learn new tricks—it's really good for them, too!

"Find something you really love and make it your career. Don't let anyone discourage you or tell you it's not practical."

—Liz Cheney

"Loneliness is the thing
to master. Courage and fear,
love, death . . . can easily
be ruled afterwards. If I
make myself master my own
loneliness there will be peace
or safety: and perhaps these
are the same."

—Martha Gellhorn

"You need a core inside you—a core that directs everything you do. You confer with it for guidance. It is not negotiable."

—Barbara Jordan

"When one door of happiness closes, another opens; but often we look so long at the closed door that we do not see the one which has been opened for us."

—Helen Keller

"All of us have to learn how to invent our lives, make them up, imagine them. We need to be taught these skills; we need guides to show us how. If we don't, our lives get made up for us by other people."

—Ursula K. Le Guin

"Passion comes after you put in the hard work to become excellent at something valuable, not before. In other words, what you do for a living is much less important than how you do it."

—Cal Newport

We all make mistakes. And that's okay. Yet many of us compound that mistake by letting it linger instead of apologizing or making it right. This also saps our energy and creativity, leaving us with less space for inspiration. But you can change that. Apologies are effective if you have the right tools. Try this simple three-step process:

ACKNOWLEDGE YOUR ACTION. This starts with saying, "I am sorry that I _____." Do not apologize for someone else's feelings; own what you did! Apologize for your actions.

ACKNOWLEDGE THE IMPACT OF YOUR ACTION. Then, say, "When I _____, I think I may have made you feel _____." Put yourself in their place and consider if your action made them feel left out, embarrassed, scared, etc.

ASK FOR THE OPPORTUNITY TO REPAIR. Ask, "How can I make this up to you?" This question puts the person you've wronged in control, and lets them tell you how you can address it (if possible). It might not be fixable, but ideally you can move toward a repair.

When you apologize, you may be able to alleviate some guilt, shame, or embarrassment, and possibly repair the relationship. In the end, it lightens your mental load and restores balance and trust in relationships.

"We do not think ourselves into new ways of living, we live ourselves into new ways of thinking."

—Richard Rohr

"Remember that if you really want to motivate yourself, love is more powerful than fear."

—Kristin Neff

"Make new
mistakes every
day. Don't waste
time repeating the
old ones."

—Danny Meyer

"You demand respect and you'll get it. First of all, you give respect."

—Mary J. Blige

"*Most of us lead far more meaningful lives than we know. Often finding meaning is not about doing things differently; it is about seeing familiar things in new ways.*"

—Rachel Naomi Remen

"Our potential is
one thing. What we do
with it is quite another."

—ANGELA DUCKWORTH

Celebrations are often associated with large-scale occasions or big milestones like national holidays, birthdays, anniversaries, and graduations. But don't forget to celebrate your everyday accomplishments, too. When you celebrate personal achievements, you're laying the foundation for future successes.

Here's how to celebrate responsibly:

SHARE THE MOMENT: Every achievement has a supporting team—someone else is always there. Watch Academy Award speeches or read the acknowledgments from a book and you'll understand that everything we do involves others.

REVIEW THE ACTIONS THAT LED YOU TO THIS MOMENT: When we make a mistake, we often play that tape on repeat in our minds. "If only I would have . . ." Remember to play the positive tape as well. Reflect on the ideas and actions you took that affected the outcome. What behaviors can you repeat in the future?

LET YOUR POSITIVE EMOTIONS FLOW: Take a beat to savor all that went into this achievement, and let yourself feel all of the feels. This is delightful in and of itself, and sets you up so that you're better prepared to do it again.

"Being trapped by fear is a form of delusion. Either I can do something or I can't. If I truly can't . . . I don't do it. If I truly can . . . I push myself."

—Sylvia Boorstein

"There are far, far better things ahead than any we leave behind."

—C. S. Lewis

"Our greatest glory consists
not in never falling, but in
rising every time we fall."

—Oliver Goldsmith

"I close my eyes with the blessed consciousness that I have left one shining track upon the earth."

—Ludwig van Beethoven

"Quant à l'avenir, votre tâche n'est pas de le prévoir mais de le permettre."

"As for the future, your task is not to imagine it, but to allow it."

—Antoine de Saint-Exupéry

"When risk is a challenge, fear becomes a compass—literally pointing people in the direction they need to go next."

—Steven Kotler

Compassion is the fine art of being present and holding space for another person to process their experience. It's sitting with someone while they experience strong, and often uncomfortable, emotions. You don't take on their feelings, attempt to change them, or problem-solve. You simply hold space.

You may have experienced sharing compassion when you've attended a funeral or a wake, or sat shiva. Sometimes you know the departed and mourn the loss you feel, and sometimes you've never met the departed but are there for those who have.

Compassion is holding space for another to fill. Technically speaking, you aren't doing anything, and yet in some ways you're doing everything. By making room for another person's challenging experience, you can help them process and feel less alone. And that can make all the difference.

"We are the ones
that we've been
waiting for."

—June Jordan

"Don't ask what the world needs. Ask what makes you come alive, and go do that, because what the world needs is people who have come alive."

—Howard Thurman

"There is nothing more beautiful than finding your course . . . This path does not belong to your parents, your teachers, your leaders, or your lovers. Your path is your character defining itself more and more every day . . ."

—Jodie Foster

"The first hour of the
morning is the rudder
of the day."

—Henry Ward Beecher

128

"Don't think in the morning. That's a big mistake that people make. They wake up in the morning and they start thinking. Don't think. Just execute the plan."

—Jocko Willink

"I also think you should embrace what you don't know, especially in the beginning, because what you don't know can become your greatest asset. It ensures that you will absolutely be doing things different from everybody else."

—Sara Blakely

As mentioned on page 124, compassion is a powerful tool for connection. People are wired to help others if they're hurt or struggling. In addition to using compassion as a tool to support others, it's also important to be compassionate with yourself. Although self-compassion doesn't come easily to many, it can be learned. These skills can help you be good to yourself:

GET PHYSICAL: Whether it's eating healthy, exercising, getting a massage, or taking a midafternoon nap, make conscious decisions that do your body good.

OWN YOUR FEELINGS: If you're upset with yourself, calmly review the situation and assess how it made you feel. You can even write yourself a letter—just don't shame or blame yourself in the process.

BEFRIEND YOURSELF: Feeling down? Just scored a big win? Think about what you'd say to a friend in a similar situation and then say it to yourself.

DEEP THOUGHTS: A consistent practice of mindfulness helps you go easier on yourself and changes your "self-talk" to one of encouragement and empathy.

"Go to the edge
of the cliff and jump
off. Build your wings
on the way down."

—Ray Bradbury

"What you do makes a difference, and you have to decide what kind of difference you want to make."

—Jane Goodall

"Each one of us has at our fingertips, access to so much meaning and hope, goodness and beauty, in every moment, if we would only let ourselves see."

—John Sean Doyle

"You just can't beat the person who never gives up."

—George Herman "Babe" Ruth

"Yes, I am a dreamer. For a dreamer is one who can find his way by moonlight, and see the dawn before the rest of the world."

—Oscar Wilde

"Never dull your shine
for somebody else."

—Tyra Banks

There are two categories of inspiration: observer and participant. As an observer, you are inspired by others' achievements. This might include watching an Olympic athlete perform, or listening to an incredible guitar solo at a concert. Parents love watching their child take those first steps; it's a landmark occasion.

You can also feel inspired when you engage or participate in an activity. You may find inspiration in your garden, cultivating the way the plants grow, shaping their future. You can dance to music instead of just listening to it, engaging with it and letting it inhabit you physically. When you watch a fireworks display, you lean back, look up into the sky, listen to the booms and fizzles, and see the lights coming and going; it's a lived experience. You can even smell the sulfur and feel the power of the explosion in your body. It's a multisensory inspirational experience that must be lived to be fully experienced.

To curate inspiration, be sure to pursue a mix of both observation and participation.

"Believe in yourself
and there will come
a day when others will
have no choice but to
believe with you."

—Cynthia Kersey

"When we live afraid to fail, we don't take risks. We don't bring our entire selves to the table—so we end up failing before we even begin."

—Abby Wambach

"Risks must be taken because the greatest hazard in life is to risk nothing."

—Leo Buscaglia

"Aerodynamically, the bumble bee shouldn't be able to fly, but the bumble bee doesn't know it so it goes on flying anyway."

—Mary Kay Ash

"Your time is way too valuable to be wasting on people that can't accept who you are."

—Turcois Ominek

". . . everything can be taken from a man but one thing: the last of the human freedoms—to choose one's attitude in any given set of circumstances, to choose one's own way."

—Viktor Frankl

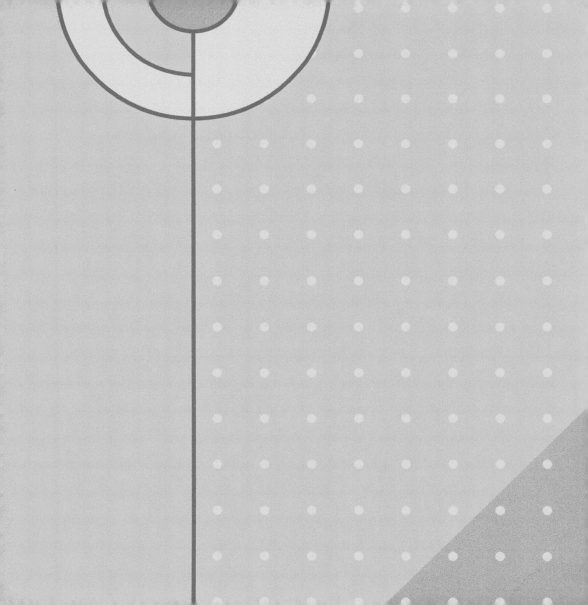

REFERENCES

Adderholdt, Miriam, and Jan Goldberg. *Perfectionism: What's Bad About Being Too Good?* Minneapolis: Free Spirit Publishing, 1987, p. 85.

Albright, Madeline. *Madam Secretary: A Memoir*. New York: Harper Perennial, 2003, p. 512.

Alexander, Kelly, and Cynthia Harris. *Hometown Appetites: The Story of Clementine Paddleford, the Forgotten Food Writer Who Chronicled How America Ate*. New York: Gotham Books, 2008.

Ali, Muhammad, Post Fight press conference [Video], March 9, 1971.

Andrews, Julie. *Home: A Memoir of My Early Years.* New York: Hachette Books, 2008.

Angelou, Maya. *Rainbow in the Cloud: The Wisdom and Spirit of Maya Angelou*. New York: Random House, 2014, p. 68.

Armstrong, Louis. "What a Wonderful World." New York: ABC Records, 1970.

Ash, Mary Kay. *Miracles Happen*. New York: William Morris Books, 2003.

Baez, Joan. *Daybreak.* Wales: Panther Publishing, 1968, pg 135.

Bailie, Gil. *Violence Unveiled.* New York: Herder & Herder, 1996, p. xv.

Beecher, Henry Ward. *Life Thoughts: Gathered from the Extemporaneous Discourses of Henry Ward Beecher*. Boston: Phillips, Sampson, 1858.

Berry, Wendell. *Farming: A Handbook.* Berkeley, CA: Counterpoint Press, 2011.

Boorstein, Sylvia. *Pay Attention, for Goodness' Sake: Practicing the Perfections of the Heart—The Buddhist Path of Kindness.* New York: Ballantine Books, 2002.

Bradbury, Ray. Speech at Brown University. *Brown Daily Herald* March 24, 1995

Brandeis, Louis. "The Opportunity in the Law," Cambridge, MA: *39 American Law Review*, May 4, 1905.

Brault, Robert. *Short Thoughts for the Long Haul.* Self-published, CreateSpace, 2017.

Brent, Samuel Arthur. *Familiar Short Sayings of Great Men.* Boston: Ticknor and Co., 1887; Bartleby.com, 2012. bartleby.com/344.

Brink, Randall. *Lost Star: The Search for Amelia Earhart*. New York: W.W. Norton & Co., 1995, p. 85.

Brooks, Gwendolyn. *Gottschalk and the Grande Tarantelle.* Chicago: The David Company, 1988.

Brunson, Michael. TV Interview for ITV, November 30, 1984.

Buck, Pearl S. *A Bridge for Passing.* New York: John Day, 1962.

Burghardt, Walter. *To Be Just Is to Love: Homilies for a Church Renewing*. Mahwah, NJ: Paulist Press, 2001, p. 214.

Buscaglia, Leo. *Living Loving and Learning.* New York: Ballantine Books, 1983.

Carr, Glynda C. "Unbought and Unbossed, Shirley Chisholm Stands as a Timely Lesson on Claiming a Seat at the Table." Huffington Post. November 30, 2017. huffpost.com/entry/unbought-and-unbossed-shirley -chisholm-stands-as-a_b_5a200c23e4b02edd56c6d71d.

Chambers, Veronica. "The Joy of Doing Things Badly." Interview by Ed Gordon. News & Notes, NPR, May 11, 2006. npr.org/templates /story/story.php?storyId=5398003.

CNN. "Youth Poet Laureate Amanda Gorman's Inaugural Poem," Jan. 20, 2021. cnn.com/2021/01/20/politics/amanda-gorman-inaugural -poem-transcript/index.html.

Collins, Marva. *Marva Collins Way.* New York: TarcherPerigee, 1990, p. 19.

Dean, Nicole. "The Importance of Novelty." *Brain World*. September 5, 2019. brainworldmagazine.com/the-importance-of-novelty/.

Doyle, Glennon. *Untamed.* New York: Dial Press, 2020.

Doyle, John Sean. *Being Human.* Self-published, 2015.

Duckworth, Angela. *Grit: The Power of Passion and Perseverance.* Simon and Schuster, 2016.

Elrod, Hal. *The Miracle Morning: The Not-So-Obvious Secret Guaranteed to Transform Your Life.* Austin: Hal Elrod International, 2012.

Emerson, Ralph Waldo. *Self-Reliance and Other Essays: Emerson's Essays, First Series.* Independently Published, 2020.

Exupéry, Antoine de Saint. *Citadelle* or *The Wisdom of the Sands.* Moscow: AST Publishers, 2004.

Faber, Barry. *Diamond Power: Gems of Wisdom from America's Greatest Marketer.* Career Pr Inc., 2003, p. 53.

Fort Worth Star-Telegram. "Pertinent Proverbs by William A. Ward." Quote Page 4-D, Column 6, May 26, 1967.

Foster, Jodie. University of Pennsylvania Commencement, 2006. "The Journey of Your Life Has a Way of Sneaking Off the Starting Line."

Frankl, Victor. *Man's Search for Meaning.* New York: Beacon Press, 2006.

Frost, Joe L. "Neuroscience, Play, and Child Development." ERIC. May 31, 1998. eric.ed.gov/?q=Neuroscience%2c+Play%2c+and+Child+Development&id=ED427845.

Gach, Gary. *The Complete Idiot's Guide to Understanding Buddhism.* New York: Alpha, 2002, p. 285.

Gaille, Brandon. "41 Priceless Cal Newport Quotes." April 21, 2015. brandongaille.com/41-priceless-cal-newport-quotes.

Gebhart, Tim. "Painter Akiane Kramarik on Her Art and Spiritual Journey," *The Epoch Times,* January 17, 2018. theepochtimes.com/painter-akiane-kramarik-on-her-art-and-spiritual-journey_2410199.html.

Gibby-Brown, Sckylar. "Robin Arzón Quotes to Inspire You to Get Up and Run." January 13, 2021. everydaypower.com/robin-arzon-quotes.

Ginsburg, Kenneth R. "The Importance of Play in Promoting Healthy Child Development and Maintaining Strong Parent-Child Bonds." *Pediatrics* 119, no. 1 (Jan 2007): 182-191. DOI: 10.1542/peds.2006-2697.

Goggins, David. *Can't Hurt Me: Master Your Mind and Defy the Odds.* Carson City: LionCrest Publishing, 2018.

Goldsmith, Oliver, *Citizen of the world: or, letters from a Chinese philosopher, residing in London, to his friends in the east,* Dublin: printed for George and Alex. Ewing, 1762. quod.lib.umich.edu/e/ecco /004776950.0001.001?view=toc.

Hare, Julius Charles, and Augustus William Hare. *Guesses at Truth by Two Brothers. Vol. 1.* London: John Taylor, 1827.

Harvard Health. "The Ideal Stretching Routine." February 3, 2021. health.harvard.edu/staying-healthy/the-ideal-stretching-routine.

Harvard Health. "The Power of Self-Compassion." June 27, 2013. health.harvard.edu/healthbeat/the-power-of-self-compassion.

Heiling, Joe. "800 Turn Out for Baseball Dinner," *The Houston Post.* January 30, 1971, p. 1-B.

Hedstrom, Deborah. *From Telegraph to Light Bulb with Thomas Edison.* Nashville: B&H Publishing, 2007, p. 22.

Howatt, William A. "The Evolution of Reality Therapy to Choice Theory." *International Journal of Reality Therapy*, 2001. msutexas.edu/academics /education/_assets/files/international_journal_of_reality_therapy _fall2001.pdf.

International Journal of Environmental Research and Public Health 17, no. 23 (2020): 8984. doi.org/10.3390/ijerph17238984.

International Journal of Reality Therapy, 2001. msutexas.edu/academics /education/_assets/files/international_journal_of_reality_therapy _fall2001.pdf.

Isaacson, Walter. *Einstein: His Life and Universe.* New York: Simon & Schuster, 2007.

Jordan, Michael. *I Can't Accept Not Trying : Michael Jordan on the Pursuit of Excellence.* San Francisco, CA: HarperSanFrancisco, 1994. p. 129.

Jordan, June. "Poem for South African Women," *Passion: New Poems, 1977–1980.* Boston, MA: Beacon Press, 1980.

The Journal of the Institution of Municipal & County Engineers, 64, no. 16 (February 1, 1938). Quotation is contained in the remarks of "Mr. Percy

Morris (Wakefield)," page 1277. Published at the Offices of the Institution of Municipal & County Engineers, London.

Kantrowitz, Barbara, and Holly Peterson. "What I Learned: Whether They're Running Universities, Political Campaigns or Major Corporations, These 11 Remarkable Women Have Found Their Own Ways of Overcoming Obstacles." *Newsweek*, October 15, 2007.

Keller, Hellen. *We Bereaved.* London: Forgotten Books, 2017.

Kessler, Ted. "Happy Landings." *The Guardian*. July 27, 2002. theguardian.com/theobserver/2002/jul/28/features.magazine27.

Khan, Janaya Future. "Our Job Is to Make Revolution Irresistible." Time: The New American Revolution. time.com/5880960/janaya-future-khan-black-lives-matter/.

Kierkegaard, Søren. *The Concept of Anxiety: A Simple Psychologically Orienting Deliberation on the Dogmatic Issue of Hereditary Sin.* Princeton: Princeton University Press, 1981.

Kiyosaki, Robert. Forward to *The Miracle Morning: The Not-So-Obvious Secret Guaranteed to Transform Your Life*. by Hal Elrod. Austin: Hal Elrod International, 2012 , xiii.

Kline, Nancy. *Time To Think: Listening to Ignite the Human Mind.* London: Cassell Publishing, 2015.

Knechtle, Beat, Zbigniew Waśkiewicz, Caio V. Sousa, Lee Hill, and Pantelis T. Nikolaidis. "Cold Water Swimming—Benefits and Risks: A Narrative

Review" *International Journal of Environmental Research and Public Health* 17, no. 23 (2020): 8984. doi.org/10.3390/ijerph17238984.

Kotler, Steven. *The Rise of Superman.* Seattle: New Harvest, 2014.
Le Guin, Ursula K. *The Wave in the Mind: Talks and Essays on the Writer, the Reader, and the Imagination.* Boulder: Shambhala, 2004.

Lawley, Sue. "Stephen Hawking, Reith Lecture 2: Black Holes Ain't as Black as They Are Painted." BBC Radio 4. 2005. downloads.bbc.co.uk/radio4/transcripts/2015_Reith_Lecture_Hawking_ep2.pdf.

Lee, Bruce, and John Tuttle (Ed.). *Striking Thoughts: Bruce Lee's Wisdom for Daily Living.* Clarendon, VT: Tuttle Publishing, 2000, p. 121.

Lesser, Elizabeth. *Broken Open: How Difficult Times Help Us Grow.* New York: Villard Publishing, 2004.

Lewis, C. S. *The Collected Letters of C. S. Lewis, Volume 3.* New York: HarperOne, 2007.

Lorimer, George Horace. *More Letters from a Self-Made Merchant to His Son.* New York: Sears, 1927.

Mahone, Austin. *Austin Mahone: Just How It Happened: My Official Story.* New York: Little, Brown and Company, 2014.

Mailer, Norman. *Of a Fire on the Moon.* New York: Random House, 1970.

Mandela, Nelson. *Nelson Mandela By Himself: The Authorised Book of Quotations*. The Nelson Mandela Foundation, 2010.

Mather, Victor, and Danielle Allentuck. "Megan Rapinoe Steals the Show at the Women's World Cup Parade." *The New York Times*. July 10, 2019. nytimes.com/2019/07/10/sports/soccer/soccer-parade.html.

Marie Martin, Rachel. *The Brave Art of Motherhood: Fight Fear, Gain Confidence, and Find Yourself Again*. Colorado Springs: WaterBrook & Multnomah Publishing, 2018.

Mason, John. *Conquering an Enemy Called Average.* Tulsa: Insight Publishing, 1996.

Mattiessen, F.O., and Kenneth Henry James Murdock. *The Notebooks of Henry James.* Chicago: The University of Chicago Press, 1981.

McGonigal, Jane. *Reality Is Broken: Why Games Make Us Better and How They Can Change the World.* New York: Penguin Books, 2011.

Meyers, Danny. *Setting the Table: The Transforming Power of Hospitality in Business.* New York: Ecco Press, 2008.

Moorehead, Caroline. *Gellhorn : A Twentieth Century Life*. New York: Henry Holt & Co., 2003, p. 88.

Montero-Marín, Jesús, Sonia Asún, Nerea Estrada-Marcén, Rosario Romero, and Roberto Asún. "Effectiveness of a Stretching Program on Anxiety Levels of Workers in a Logistic Platform: A Randomized Controlled Study." *Atencion Primaria* 45, no. 7 (Aug–Sep 2013):376–383. DOI: 10.1016/j.aprim.2013.03.002.

Moses, Grandma *Grandma Moses : My Life's History.* New York Harper & Brothers, 1952.

Murakami, Haruki. *Kafka on the Shore.* New York: Knopf, 2005.

Niven, David, PhD. *The 100 Simple Secrets of Successful People (What Scientists Have Learned and How You Can Use It).* New York: HarperOne, 2006.

Nyad, Diana. *Find a Way.* New York: Vintage, 2016.

Ominek, Turcois. *Masquerade: A Collection of Thoughts Affected by Love.* Self-published, 2013.

Paiella, Gabriella. "How I Get It Done: Brené Brown, Author and Research Professor at the University of Houston." The Cut. April 22, 2019. thecut.com/2019/04/how-i-get-it-done-bren-brown-research-professor.html.

Philip, Benjamin A., Scott H. Frey. and Mark P. McAvoy. "Interhemispheric Parietal-Frontal Connectivity Predicts the Ability to Acquire a Nondominant Hand Skill." *Brain Connectivity*. 11, no. 4 (May 2021): 308–318. doi.org/10.1089/brain.2020.0916.

Pierce, Paula Jo. *Let Me Tell You What I've Learned: Texas Wisewomen Speak.* Austin: University of Texas Press, 2010, p. 17.

Pritchard, David, and Alan Lysaght. *The Beatles: An Oral History*. New York: Lysaght, 1998, p. 285.

Remen, Rachel Naomi. *My Grandfather's Blessings: Stories of Strength, Refuge, and Belonging.* New York: Riverheard Books, 2001.

Robinson, Jackie. "Why 'I Never Had It Made': Jackie Robinson's Own Story," *Newsday*. November 5, 1972.

Rohr, Richard. *Everything Belongs: The Gift of Contemplative Prayer.* Chestnut Ridge, NY: The Crossroad Publishing Company, 2003, p. 17-20.

Roosevelt, Eleanor. *You Learn By Living: 11 Keys for a More Fulfilling Life.* New York: Harper Perennial Modern Classics, p. 65

Rumi, Jelaluddin. *The Glance: Songs of Soul-Meeting.* Translated by Coleman Barks. New York: Viking Penguin, 1999.

Ruth, George Herman, *The Rotarian, "Bat It Out!",* Rotary International, July 1940, p. 14.

Sagan, Carl. "The Burden of Skepticism." *Skeptical Inquirer* 12, no. 1 (Fall 1987).

San Antonio Light. "What They're Saying," p. 28, May 18, 1977. newspaperarchive.com/san-antonio-light-may-18-1977-p-28.

Shenker, Israel. "Mrs. Meir, at Princeton, Offers Her Views in Talks Marked by Humor and Grimness," *The New York Times*. December 12, 1974 nytimes.com/1974/12/12/archives/mrs-meir-at-princeton-offers-her-views-in-talks-marked-by-humor-and.html?searchResultPosition=1.

Sherman, Karen J., Rachel M. Ceballos, Daniel C. Cherkin, Andrea J. Cook, and Robert D. Wellman. "Mediators of Yoga and Stretching for Chronic Low Back Pain." *Hindawi*. vol. 2013 (2013). doi.org/10.1155/2013/130818.

Smith, Bodhi. "Sunbathers," [Photo]. BodhiSmith.com. bodhismith.com /bodhi-blog/blog_posts/sunbathers-by-bodhi-smith.

Sonnier, Suzanne. *Dolly Parton: In Her Own Words.* Evanston, Il: Agate Publishing, 2020.

Success Resources. "Sara Blakely's Top 5 Startup Tips." Facebook, May 20, 2020. facebook.com/watch/?v=3033790576644016.

TED.com. "Before Avatar . . . a Curious Boy." James Cameron. 2010 TED Conference, Long Beach, February 13, 2010. ted.com/talks/james _cameron_before_avatar_a_curious_boy.

The New York Times. "Full Text of Bush's [Republican National Convention] Acceptance Speech," August 4, 2000. nytimes.com/library/politics /camp/080400wh-bush-speech.html.

Trump, Ivanka. *Women Who Work: Rewriting the Rules for Success*. New York: Portfolio, 2017.

Tyson, Neil deGrasse, with James Trefil. *Cosmic Queries: StarTalk's Guide to Who We Are, How We Got Here, and Where We're Going.* National Geographic, 2021.

US Navy Admiral William H. McRaven, University of Texas at Austin Commencement Address, May 19, 2014.

Venstra, Elizabeth. *True Genius: 1001 Quotes That Will Change Your Life.* New York: SkyHorse Publishing, 2008.

Walsh, Colleen. "Honoring Ruth Bader Ginsburg." *The Harvard Gazette.* May 29, 2015. news.harvard.edu/gazette/story/2015/05/honoring-ruth-bader-ginsburg.

Wambach, Ally. *WOLFPACK: How to Come Together, Unleash Our Power, and Change the Game.* New York: Celadon Books, 2019.

Williams, Brian. "Jobs: Iconoclast and Salesman." MSNBC. May 25, 2006.

Willink, Jocko. *Discipline Equals Freedom: Field Manual.* New York: St. Martin's Press, 2017.

Winfrey, Oprah. *The Path Made Clear: Discovering Your Life's Direction and Purpose.* New York: Flatiron Press, 2019.

Winnicott, Donald Woods. *Playing and Reality: D.W. Winnicott.* London: Tavistock, 1971.

Yousafzai, Malala. *The Daily Show.* Octobert 10, 2013. youtube.com/watch?v=gjGL6YY6oMs.

ACKNOWLEDGMENTS

We'd like to thank Callisto for giving us the opportunity to partner on this book. Thank you to our children for giving us the time to write it, and our communities for your support and inspiration. We thank those who've come before us and shared their wisdom so that we could capture it and share it with you.

ABOUT THE AUTHORS

ALLISON and **AARON TASK** live between Montclair, New Jersey, and Lake Naomi, Pennsylvania, with their children and pets. Aaron is an award-winning journalist, and Allison is a career and life coach, and best-selling author. They wake up early.

CPSIA information can be obtained
at www.ICGtesting.com
Printed in the USA
JSHW010033241121
R11310000001B/R113100PG20693JSX00001B/1

9 781638 073628